Aural Time!

Practice Tests for ABRSM and other Exams

Grade 7

DAVID TURNBULL

CONTENTS

Bosworth

INTRODUCTION

Aural training has always been of the greatest importance to teachers and their pupils. In recent years the emphasis has changed from dependence on memory to the development of a wider sense of musical awareness.

The Associated Board of the Royal Schools of Music revised its aural tests for Grades 1–5 in 1993 (with some further changes in Grades 4 and 5 in 1995). New tests are being introduced for Grades 6, 7 and 8 from January, 1996.

Like most musical skills, aural awareness needs regular training and practice. Aural work should be part of every lesson. Teachers may like to use this book to supplement the aural training material they devise for themselves.

The 1996 tests for Grade 7 include tests in sight singing a melody above a played bass. Sight singing of any sort — the basis of so much musical training and enjoyment — has been neglected in musical education in the last few decades. Pupils will therefore need considerable practice to achieve the necessary standard. Pupils may be also find another book in the *Aural Time!* series useful. *Easy Sight Singing & Voice Pitching Practice*, (Bosworth Edition 4801), contains 70 short examples of accompanied sight-singing suitable for a beginner, in a variety of major and minor keys.

The material in this book will be found useful not only for ABRSM examinations. The skills developed by its use will be of considerable help to candidates for GCSE and A level, and for all musicians who wish to improve their general musical awareness.

Most of the examples in this book have been taken from the works of established composers. In many cases examples have been adapted or transposed to make them more useful for their present purpose. This is particularly true of examples which have to be sung.

As always, I am grateful to my wife for her constant help and encouragement.

David Turnbull
Solihull, August 1995

Uniform with this volume: *Aural Time!* Grades 1–6 (already published). Pupil's book for Grades 4 & 5. *Aural Time! Easy Sight Singing & Voice Pitching.*

In preparation: *Aural Time!* Grade 8, Pupil's books for Grades 6, 7 and 8.

Also by David Turnbull: *Theory Time!* Step-by-step instruction in musical theory and rudiments. Grades 1–5.

All published by Bosworth & Co.

Test A. Singing or Playing from Memory

Pupils must sing or play from memory the lower part of a two-part phrase. The key-chord and the starting note will be played and named, and two bars of the pulse will be tapped. In an examination, the example will be played twice. When giving practice, however, teachers should not hesitate to play the test more frequently, and if necessary be prepared to divide the test into sections. Tests should be played at the keyboard using both hands, so that the separate lines are as clearly defined as possible. *If the example starts with a single part or a unison, the pupil must be warned.*

2

4

20 Molto moderato — Vaughan Williams

© 1921 Stainer & Bell Ltd. Reproduced by permission from "Six Short Pieces, No. 1"

21 Lebhaft — Schumann

22 Allegro — Prokofiev

© Copyright 1936 by Hawkes & Son (London) Ltd.
Reproduced by permission of
Boosey & Hawkes Music Publishers Ltd.

23 Allegro — Purcell

24 Allegro — Corelli

25 Andante — Bartók

© Copyright 1946 by Hawkes & Son (London) Ltd.
Reproduced by permission of
Boosey & Hawkes Music Publishers Ltd.

26 Andante — Bach

6

Adagio Dunstable

41

Lento Rameau (adapted)

42

Allegro ma non troppo Bach

43

Moderato Certon

44

Allegro moderato Monteverdi

45

Andante Gershwin

46

molto cantabile

Test B. Sight-Singing

Pupils should be able to sing a short melody, accompanied by a lower part played on the piano. The test may be in any major or minor key up to four sharps or flats. The key-chord and starting note will be given, and the pulse indicated.

10

12

Test C. Cadences, Cadence Chords and Modulations.

Test C1. For Grade 7, pupils must be able to recognise **interrupted** cadences in major and minor keys, as well as the **perfect** and **imperfect** cadences set in Grade 6. *In addition* —

Test C2. Pupils must be able to name the two chords which form the cadence (marked by * in the examples). These chords will be restricted to:

(a) In **root position** the chords of the tonic, subdominant, dominant, dominant seventh and submediant.

(b) In **second inversion**, the chord of the tonic.

Chords may be described either by their full name (for example, "tonic, in second inversion") or by their number and inversion (for example, "Va"). *In addition* —

Test C3. Pupils must be able to recognise the modulations described on page 20.

Interrupted cadences found in Grade 7 will be the submediant chord in root position (VIa) preceded *either* by the dominant chord in root position (Va) *or* by the dominant seventh chord in root position (V^7a).

Perfect cadences found in Grade 7 tests will be the tonic chord in root position (Ia) preceded *either* by the dominant chord in root position (Va) *or* by the dominant seventh chord in root position (V^7a).

Imperfect cadences found in Grade 7 tests will be the dominant chord in root position (Va) preceded by the tonic chord in root position (Ia) *or* the tonic chord in second inversion (Ic) *or* the subdominant chord in root position (IVa). In practice, IVa–Va is much less frequently used by composers than Ia–Va, or Ic–Va.

Pupils should be reminded that:

● at the beginning of any test, the keychord will be played. The pupil must memorise the sound of this tonic chord, and decide if the chord is major or minor.

● in minor keys, the dominant chord at cadences is major, because of the sharpened seventh;

● in major keys, the submediant chord is minor, but in minor keys the submediant chord is major.

It follows from the above that —

(i) if a phrase has been given a keychord which is major and ends with a minor chord, the cadence must be interrupted;

(ii) if a phrase has been given a keychord which is minor and ends with a minor chord, the cadence must be perfect;

● the tonic chord in second inversion (Ic) is often found as the first of the two chords of an imperfect cadence, and pupils must be able to recognise it quickly.

● dominant seventh chords are often used in cadences, and pupils must recognise quickly whether a chord is a dominant chord or a dominant seventh chord.

Some preparatory work on the points above should be done before the following examples are attempted.

Play an example chosen from one of the groups *twice*, having sounded the keychord first with its tonic doubled in the bass. Ask the pupil to name the cadence. Then play the keychord again, followed by the first of the two cadence chords. Ask its name. Then sound the second cadence chord and ask its name.

Interrupted Cadences

Andante — Handel

7

Tempo di Menuetto — Greene

8

Perfect Cadences

Allegro — Haydn

9

Tempo di Menuetto — Hook

10

Lento — English traditional

11

Andante — Schubert

12

Grazioso — Brahms

19

Lento — Farnaby

20

Langsam — Schumann

21

Imperfect Cadences

Andante cantabile — Mozart

22

Allegro non troppo — Brahms

23

Test C3 Modulations. Pupils must be able to recognise if a phrase starting in a major key has modulated to the key of its dominant major, to its subdominant major, or to its relative minor.

- Modulations to the dominant major involve a sharpening, and this produces an effect which can be described as "brightening."

- Modulations to the subdominant major involve a flattening, and this produces an effect which can be described as "darkening."

- If a Grade 7 example ends in a minor key, it has modulated to its relative minor.

It may be helpful for pupils to practice these preliminary exercises.

1 Major to dominant major

2 Major to subdominant major

3 Major to relative minor

Test C3 Modulations. The original key chord will be sounded, and then the test will be played once only.

Tonic major to Subdominant

Tonic major to Relative minor

Lento — Bach

12

Allegretto — Benda

13

Schubert

Allegro marcato

14

Andante — German traditional

15

Andantino — Georges Bull

16

from *A Petits Pas*, 25 Études mignonnes, Leduc
Reproduced by permission of Éditions Heugel et Cie., Paris /
United Music Publishers Ltd.

Tonic major to Dominant

Allegro — Schumann

17

24

Test D. Questions about Pieces

In Test D of ABRSM examinations the questions on pieces are in two parts.

D (i) Questions will be asked about the musical features of a piece, including **rhythm**, **tempo**, **melody**, **form** (including phrase structure and phrase length), **dynamics**, **articulation**, **harmony** and **texture**.

Questions may also be asked about **tonality** *and related matters*. "Related matters", particularly in examinations like A level and GCSE, could include the use of a mode rather than a key, atonality, the use of unusual scales, and also the disturbance of the sense of key by the use of chromaticism.

A consideration of these features should allow a pupil to determine the **character** of the music, and its **style** and **period**.

Choose one or two features from the list below each piece. Tell the pupil the subjects of questions before the piece is played. Parts of the piece may be repeated if necessary.

Further information may be found in the Pupil's Book for Grades 6 and 7, and in *Have I passed my Piano Exam* by David Paul Martin (Music Plaza / Bosworth).

Comments on the questions about pieces in this section are printed on Page 36.

D (ii) Pupils must clap a single-line extract taken from each piece, and be able to describe the piece as being in two, three, four or six-eight time. In examination situations, pupils will only be asked to clap one example, but to provide more practice two examples for clapping are given for each piece.

The questions in this section are useful preparation for many other types of music examination, like the GCSE. Pupils for other examinations can practise writing down *answers instead of giving them verbally.*

Allegro   Daniel Purcell

D (i) *Questions*

(a) Rhythm	What rhythmic device is used at the beginning of bars 1 and 2?
(b) Tonality, etc.	Comment on the tonality of this music. Does the tonality change?
(c) Phrase structure	Describe the phrase structure of this extract.
(d) Dynamics	Do the dynamics change? If so, gradually or suddenly?
(e) Style and period	In what style and period do you think this was composed?

D (ii) Clap one of the following extracts, and say if the piece is in two, three, four or six-eight time.

Tempo di Menuetto

Beethoven

2

D (i) *Questions*

(a) Form	Describe the form of this piece.
(b) Melody	Is the opening four-bar melodic phrase repeated?
	If so, what do you notice about the repeat?
(c) Rhythm	What rhythmic idea is present in all melodic phrases?
(d) Style and period	In which period do you think this was composed? Name a possible composer.

D (ii) Clap one of the following extracts, and say if the piece is in two, three, four or six-eight time.

D (i) *Questions*

(a) Texture   (i) Describe the texture of this music.
              (ii) How many separate parts are present by the end?
(b) Tonality, etc.   Compare the tonality at the beginning and end of this extract.
(c) Tempo   Does the tempo change, or stay the same?
(d) Form   What name is given to this type of composition?

D (ii) Clap one of the following extracts, and say if the piece is in two, three, four or six-eight time.

Simone Plé

La Chanson du Petit Mousse

Reproduced by permission of
Éditions Henry Lemoine, Paris /
United Music Publishers Ltd.

D (i) *Questions*

(a) Melody   Compare the melody in phrases 1 and 2 with the melody in phrases 3 and 4.

(b) Texture   Is the melody always in the treble? Comment.

(c) Tonality, etc.   Is this piece atonal, modal or in a minor key?

(d) Tempo   Which of the following best describes the tempo?

         (a) *Allegro non troppo*   (b) *Adagio*   (c) Unhurried

D (ii) Clap one of the following extracts, and say if the piece is in two, three, four or six-eight time.

D (i) *Questions*

(a) Melody	Compare the melody of the second half of this extract with the melody of the first half.	
(b) Texture	Compare the texture of the start of the second half of this extract with the texture of the first half.	
(c) Tempo	Does the tempo alter or stay the same?	
(d) Form	This extract is part of a dance. What sort of dance is it?	
(e) Style and period	In which style and period do you think this music was written?	

D (ii) Clap one of the following extracts, and say if the piece is in two, three, four or six-eight time.

Assai lento, ♪ = ca.125   semplice   Bartók

© Copyright 1946 by Hawkes & Son (London) Ltd.
Reproduced by permission of Boosey & Hawkes Music Publishers Ltd.

D (i)   *Questions*

(a) **Phrase structure**   How long is the opening phrase?
(b) **Dynamics**   Describe the dynamics of the piece.
(c) **Tonality**, etc.   Comment on the tonality of the last cadence.
(d) **Texture**   Describe the texture of this music.
(e) **Style and period**   In what period do you think this might this have been written?
                            Name a possible composer.

D (ii)   Clap one of the following extracts, and say if the piece is in two, three, four or six-eight time.

Bach

D (i) *Questions*

(a) Texture How many separate parts are present (i) at the beginning? (ii) at the end?
(b) Tonality, etc. Does the tonality remain the same throughout? If not, what happens?
(c) Melody Where, and in which part, did you hear a rising scale of nearly two octaves?
(d) Tempo Were there any changes to the tempo?
(e) Period In what period of music history do you think this was composed? Why?

D (ii) Clap one of the following extracts, and say if the piece is in two, three, four or six-eight time.

Langsam (♩)

Schönberg

© 1913 by Universal Edition. Reproduced by permission.

D (i)   *Questions*

(a) Articulation   Comment on the articulation of this music

(b) Dynamics   Describe the dynamics of the piece.

(c) Tonality, etc.   Is this music tonal, atonal, bitonal or modal?

(d) Tempo   Does the tempo alter. If so, how?

(e) Period   In what period of music history might this have been written?

D (ii)   Clap one of the following extracts, and say if the piece is in two, three, four or six-eight time.

D (i) *Questions*

(a) Dynamics	Where is the climax of this music? Discuss the dynamics as a whole.
(b) Tonality, etc.	Comment on the tonality of the music.
(c) Phrase structure	How often did you hear the phrase which started the music?
(d) Tempo	What tempo mark best suits this music?
(e) Style and period	What is the style and period of this music?

D (ii) Clap one of the following extracts, and say if the piece is in two, three, four or six-eight time.

D (i) *Questions*

(a) Melody   Comment on the relationship of the melody in bar 1 with that of bar 2.
(b) Form   Describe the form of this music.
(c) Texture   Comment on the texture of the music.
(d) Dynamics   Are there any sudden changes to dynamics? Comment.
(e) Period   In what period do you think this was written? Name a possible composer.

D (ii) Clap one of the following extracts, and say if the piece is in two, three, four or six-eight time.

1

2

Gibbons

D (i) *Questions*

(a) Texture   Describe the texture of this music.
(b) Form   The form is a courtly dance. Do you think it is a minuet, an allemande or a pavane?
(c) Tonality, etc. Compare the final chord with the tonality of the piece as a whole.
(d) Melody   What do you notice about the top line of the last four bars?
(e) Period   In what period do you think this was written, and for what instrument?

D (ii) Clap one of the following extracts, and say if the piece is in two, three, four or six-eight time.

Appendix. Comments on the questions on music in Test D.

The answers below are not the only possible ones.

No. 1 **(a)** Syncopation. **(b)** Minor – no change throughout. **(c)** Four four-bar phrases, all starting the same way but the second and fourth having an altered ending. **(d)** See score. **(e)** Dance style with terraced dynamics and steady tempo. Baroque.

No. 2 **(a)** Ternary, ABA (section A has two phrases, which start in the same way). **(b)** Repeated an octave higher. **(c)** Dotted quaver – semiquaver figure. **(d)** the well-balanced ("periodic") phrasing and uncomplicated ("functional") harmony suggest Classical style.

No. 3 **(a)** Contrapuntal – 3 parts by the end. **(b)** The extract starts in a major key and ends in the (relative) minor. **(c)** Stays the same. **(d)** Fugue.

No. 4 **(a)** In sequence, a third lower. **(b)** At first in the treble, but it moves to the bass before returning to the treble. **(c)** Modal. **(d)** Unhurried.

No. 5 **(a)** The melody of the second half is a decorated version of the melody of the first half. **(b)** The texture at the start of the second half is 2-part (single notes in each hand), while the first half consists of block chords. **(c)** Stays the same. **(d)** Minuet, starting on the first beat of the bar. **(e)** Well-balanced ("periodic") phrasing and uncomplicated ("functional") harmonies suggest Classical style - probably early classical as the Minuet phrases start on the first beat of the bar without an anacrusis.

No. 6 **(a)** Three bars. **(b)** See score. **(c)** Modal. **(d)** Mostly 2-part (single notes in treble and bass) but chordal ("homophonic") at cadences. **(e)** Twentieth century, suggested by the eclectic mix of modality with shifting tonal centres, irregular phrase lengths and sparse textures. The feeling of Eastern European folk music in a twentieth century idiom might suggest Bartók as the correct composer.

No. 7 **(a)** Two at the start, three at the end. **(b)** No change (despite the different inflexions arising from the use of the melodic minor). **(c)** In the bass part, in the middle of the piece. **(d)** No change. **(e)** Baroque, suggested by continuous movement driving through cadence points and the contrapuntal texture.

No. 8 **(a)** Contrast of very short staccato notes with legato. **(b)** Wide and sudden change in first right hand bars. **(c)** Atonal – the music has no fixed key centre. **(d)** See score. **(e)** The foregoing, together with the angular melodic line and use of extreme dissonance, suggest twentieth century.

No. 9 **(a)** See score. **(b)** Major, with frequent chromaticism (note, the chromatic chords are secondary dominants and not actual modulations - they twice form part of the progression known as a cycle of fifths). **(c)** Twice (the second time with a varied ending). **(d)** Andante or similar. **(e)** The chromaticism, melody-dominated texture and frequent changes in dynamics, suggest romantic style and period.

No. 10 **(a)** Sequence. **(b)** Ternary form (AA¹BA¹ – the last phrase with a two-bar extension). **(c)** First half mostly chordal ("homophonic"), but broken chords at the start of B and thicker chords at the ends of both main sections. **(d)** *sf* often used in the music, which is otherwise *piano* until the last two *forte* bars. **(e)** The clarity and balance of the writing, and the straightforward, functional harmony, suggest the classical period. Mozart or a contemporary.

No. 11 **(a)** Contrapuntal. **(b)** Pavane. A pavane is a slow dance in duple time, starting on the first beat of the bar. **(c)** The last chord forms a major ending to a mainly minor (or modal) piece (this use of the major third is known as a *Tierce de Picardie*). **(d)** The same pitch repeated (a "pedal point") in long notes. **(e)** The foregoing, together with the ornamentation of contrapuntal lines, suggests renaissance / early baroque music for the virginals or harpsichord.

Printed and bound in Great Britain by
Caligraving Limited Thetford Norfolk